3 Steps to
$10,000 a Month
in Instant
Passive Income
Streams

GIVE YOUR BOSS THE FINGER WITH THIS SHORTCUT TO FINANCIAL FREEDOM

Written By J. P. Clarke
www.jp-clarke.com

TABLE OF CONTENTS

INTRODUCTION

"If you do not find a way to make money while you sleep, you will work until you die."

- Warren Buffet

I t's Monday morning; you hate Monday mornings! Yet there you are at your job thinking to yourself, what am I doing here..? Unsatisfied, demotivated, underappreciated, stressed, and struggling to make something of your life. Finally, you decide you have had enough; you want to prove to yourself, your family, and your friends that you can become a success and live a life of purpose without the financial burden of your daily decisions resting heavily on your shoulders. You decide to take action, to educate yourself, and obtain the tools for success to force yourself to take steps to achieve your goals. You realize you cannot be stuck in the rat race any longer, living paycheck to paycheck. You find the courage to finally give your boss the finger and say those words that have so often been on the tip of your tongue in so many stressful situations - "I QUIT!" You finally get to say it; it feels exhilarating!! You walk out with the biggest smile that your face has felt in years, filled with joy and excitement. Now, what do you do...? Oh no, the fear sets in as you begin to wonder how you will support your family, but you soon realize you have taken the first step to financial freedom. You realize that through education and action, you will achieve your dreams!

You want to learn how to earn over $10,000 per month passively with very little daily input, freeing up your time to enjoy the more important things in life, such as family, friends, health, love, and everything else that is important to you without having to worry about the associated financial burden that life throws at you. This book is the next step in learning how to quickly build passive income streams to attain financial freedom and live the life you dreamed of and deserve!

I have worked hard to build the passive revenue streams I am fortunate to have today, allowing me the lifestyle and luxuries I choose. Now don't get me wrong, it isn't easy, it requires arduous work, and you will likely fail at some point. But you will also succeed, and rest assured that the number of your successes will far outweigh your failures. Through my own extensive experience in all my years of business, with constant trial and error of thousands of different money-making ideas that I have conjured up, strategies I have tried, businesses I have run and made a success of (and sometimes failure), invaluable life lessons, I am pleased that I can share with you some of my most successful strategies to generate passive income streams, requiring little to no capital outlay, focused around minimal time input in terms of the daily management of the businesses once setup - you are setup up for success when you implement what you will learn in this book.

What is passive income?

Passive income is income you generate in a manner that requires little to no daily effort to maintain. It is money that flows in regular intervals without the need to put in a considerable amount of effort or time to create it.

What is financial freedom?

To me, financial freedom means that you get to make life decisions without being concerned about the financial implications of those decisions. It is a matter of control: you control your financial freedom by having your money work for you instead of being controlled by your money and, in so doing, being forced to work for your money. We have been brought up with the old-school, outdated mentality that we have to go to work every day and slave away for hours working for an often unsatisfying paycheck. This antiquated mindset believes that the more effort and work you put in directly translates to earning more money; however, in reality, it is often the case that the more effort and work you put in, the bigger the negative impact on your life, which often coincides with little value in terms of reward. We often forget that the one thing in life we cannot buy is time. This makes – time - the most valuable commodity available to us, and we should therefore ensure that we are making the most of the little time we have available on this precious time on earth.

But how?

By working smarter, not harder, it is possible to generate multiple passive income streams allowing you to live a healthier, happier life. Now I am in no way saying there is no benefit to hard work; there are many benefits to good old-fashioned blood, sweat, and tears. It is where this hard work is spent and focussed that really matters.

According to the Bureau of Labor Statistics (BLS), the median wage for workers in the United States is $51,168 per year. Assuming the average salaried worker works 40 hours per week in the 9-5 rat race, this means they are only earning a measly $24.60 per hour.

In contrast, using the methods you will learn in this book, the goal is to spend no more than 20 hours per week on your passive income streams that will generate an income in excess of $10,000 per month. This equates to an hourly income of $115.38, equating to 469% more than the hourly wage in an average 9-5 job! Which would you rather earn??

Passive income allows us to reduce the number of hours we work whilst increasing our earnings exponentially. So why do we force ourselves to be slaves to our employers? The time to make a change is now; with the right tools, you will achieve your goals!

All you have to do is follow the step-by-step methods you will learn in this book, and most important of all - TAKE ACTION TODAY, not tomorrow, not next week, but right now!

STEP 1

GET YOUR HEAD IN THE GAME

"There can be no life without change, and to be afraid of what is different or unfamiliar is to be afraid of life."

- Theodore Roosevelt

Think better

The first step is to forget everything! Okay, maybe not everything, but for most of us, what we have been taught about money growing up is a very outdated principle of working extremely hard for someone else for our whole lives, saving our money in the bank, and planning for retirement. Whilst this strategy may work for some, it is not an effective way of thinking about money in the 21st century. If you want a fast track to financial freedom, then you need to start thinking about money differently.

Work smarter, not harder

By starting to work smarter, spending less time on tedious tasks, and instead, using the money you earn to make more money so that your money works for you rather than you working for your money; not allowing it to collect dust in a low interest-bearing bank account for years, you will be able to achieve your goals a lot quicker. We will also start to adopt more of a problem-solving mindset where we will find ourselves challenging the common statements such as "I can't afford that" to better thought-provoking statements such as "How can I afford that?" Moving forward, when we want to buy something, we need to shift the idea from whether or not we can afford it to what passive income revenue stream we can create in order that we can afford it.

Debt is good

We have been taught for years to save all of our money in a bank for a rainy day. Now whilst it is a good idea to have a little money tucked away for a rainy day in the event of an emergency, it is also a good idea to ensure that we take advantage of the resources we have available to us, whether it be funds that we have saved up in our bank accounts, or even making use of debt available to us in order to give us a boost to where we need to get to. Do not be afraid of debt! Making use of low-cost or free debt is a fantastic way to get a step up, especially if your bank account balance is not looking too shabby right now! The antiquated idea that we should not use other people's money, such as bank loans, credit cards, or borrowing from friends and family, is another mindset change we all need to make. In order to fast-track our progress, we need to make use of all the resources available to us, so long as we are doing so responsibly.

I encourage you to make use of all the resources available to you, as when we do so, it will be on the basis of a clear strategy of how that investment is going to impact your business, how much money it will return in profit, and in what timescale this will occur, which will allow us to ensure the return of those funds which will result in a benefit to all parties involved.

Time is precious - Outsource!

Do you understand the value of your time? Time is one of the most important commodities we have available to us, we have a very limited amount of time available to us, and we, therefore, need to ensure that in our everyday lives, we are as efficient as possible so as to ensure that what we are spending our time on when it comes to business and making money, are those specific tasks that are going to generate revenue for us. All the other minuscule tasks that take up a lot of your time but which serve no direct impact on revenue generation can be outsourced or delegated. The goal will be for you to eventually get a virtual assistant, who offers high-quality work at very affordable costs, that can complete the time-consuming and less productive tasks on your behalf so that you can ensure you are focusing your time on only the most important aspects of your business, and in so doing, reduce your overall working hours to a maximum of 20 hours per week. Having a virtual assistant is a great way of taking advantage of the benefits of a highly-skilled, worldwide workforce, which are available to us at a fraction of the cost, starting at around $4 per hour. They can take care of everything from customer inquiries, Facebook & Google advertising, order fulfillment, general administrative tasks, call handling, scheduling, and so much more.

"You don't build a business, you build people, then people build the business."

- Zig Ziglar

Fiverr.com & Upwork.com are fantastic websites where you will be able to outsource almost any task you could ever think of. So wherever you lack in skill, willingness, or ability, these sites make it easy to bridge the gap with the perfect freelancer. Rather than hiring various people for individual jobs, I find it more cost-effective to source an all-rounder virtual assistant that has a diverse skill set that meets many needs in my businesses. Make a list of areas of expertise you need assistance with, whether it be graphic design, sales & marketing, I.T. & communications, or even general admin, and then align this within your hiring process to find the best person for the job. You could also outsource on a per-project basis. Due to exchange rate differences and lower costs of living in various countries worldwide, you will often be able to secure highly skilled freelancers at unbelievable rates who will do a great job. Read their reviews and ask for references.

For the purposes of the strategies that we will implement in this book, virtual assistants are highly effective at carrying out the day-to-day tasks of running your business. Learning to delegate effectively is an essential part of running any business.

STEP 2
CHOOSE YOUR STRATEGIES

"A vision without a strategy remains an illusion."

- Lee Bolman

There are many ways to reach $10,000+ per month. Here are 8 different passive income strategies you can adopt today to get you started in reaching your goal. Each of these methods is a proven strategy I have used, which can provide substantial passive income streams if you work at them diligently; which of these you choose is entirely up to you! I provide a basic outline of each strategy to give you enough information for you to decide which is the right fit for you, providing a firm foothold so that you can go out and learn more about each of them to implement into your $10,000 per month goal.

Choosing the right strategies can be hard for some; what I recommend you do is run through all of the strategies and start with the ones that align best with the interests and hobbies you enjoy the most. Business is all about doing what you love, so it is best to start with the ones which you think you may enjoy the most. When it comes to business, it is always best to diversify as much as possible, but also not to overwhelm yourself. If you are the kind of person that tends to lose focus easily or is unable to multi-task effectively, then it may be best that you start with one or two strategies and then work your way up from there. If you are someone who can manage a lot on your plate all at the same time, then feel free to take on a few more. However, it is better to be a master of one than a master of none, so if in doubt, start with one strategy, then go from there.

DROPSHIPPING

"Whatever the mind can conceive and believe,
the mind can achieve."

\- Napoleon Hill

What is Dropshipping?

Dropshipping is a retail fulfillment method where a dropshipping store (an eCommerce website you create) doesn't keep the products it sells in stock. Instead, when making a sale on your website to a customer, you purchase the item from a third party, and the third party packages and ships it directly to your customer. As a result, you never have to handle the product directly. You also never need to pay for any stock upfront; you receive your money from your customer before you buy any stock!

The biggest difference between dropshipping and the standard retail model is that the seller (you) doesn't stock or own inventory. Instead, you purchase inventory as needed from a third party—usually a dropshipping wholesaler or manufacturer—to fulfill orders. You are an intermediary between your customer and your dropshipping supplier.

All you need to do is source best-selling products, advertise them for sale on your website, and establish a relationship with a dropshipping supplier who takes care of the fulfillment for you. The supplier has no interest in promoting their branding to your customer; their concern is simply with volume sales.

Let's say, for example, you want to sell a pet bed on your store. You can source this from the dropshipping supplier for around $10, including shipping to your customer, you sell it on your website for $50, and you make a profit of $40 on each sale. You keep the $50, and you pay $10 to the supplier to get the product to your customer. I have personally run a store in the pet niche, which was generating in excess of $15,000 per month selling a single product, a super-soft pet bed, to my customers in the USA, Canada, UK & Australia. It only required 15 mins of my time each day when I was doing all the work myself; I later outsourced these tasks to my virtual assistant and was then generating $15,000 per month with zero daily input into the business!

For under $100, including store setup and a little advertising, you can get your store set up and running within a couple of hours, generating an immediate income.

Dropshipping is a really great business model if you do not want to invest loads of money into buying & holding stock. It all comes down to great product selection and good advertising and marketing. You do not need to rent any costly warehouse or shop front space and you can run this business from the comfort of your home. You do not need a lot of money to get started, and you can get fully set up in just a few hours and start making money immediately. Once you have set up your store, you will literally only need to spend around 15 mins a day on the store to manage order fulfillment & customer queries. When I first started my dropshipping stores, I simply spent 10-15 mins each morning on them; at the click of a button, I got the orders fulfilled and then responded to a couple of emails. Now that I run a multitude of successful stores generating hundreds of orders each day, I delegate the order fulfillment and customer queries to my virtual assistant, so I don't need to spend any time on it at all.

Case study

If you have ever heard of Wayfair.com, you may be surprised to learn that this is the perfect example of a successful eCommerce furniture dropshipping store. Wayfair started as a dropshipping business when it was founded in 2002 as CSN Stores. After analyzing the market, they decided to sell stereo racks and stands online. They created 250 standalone sites in different niches, which they later merged into Wayfair in 2011. Wayfair sources its products from thousands of dropship suppliers (around 95% of their products). Wayfair also offers a dropship supply program, so you can use them as a supplier to dropship their products to your customers.

Steps to immediate passive income with Dropshipping:

- ***Source best-selling products***

  There are many ways to source products. The easiest way would be to find the best-selling products on Aliexpress.com; this is a directory of manufacturers located all over the world that supply products worldwide. You can choose a niche that you would like to be in, for instance, the pet niche, then search or browse products sorting them in order of the highest number of orders. Select either one product or a few different products to later import into your store. Other ways to source products are by searching Google trends or best sellers on popular sites such as Amazon, Wish, Kickstarter, etc., or by researching the latest trending Facebook video ads, which are usually where most dropshipping products are advertised. Below is a list of the most popular dropship suppliers:

  - Spocket

  - AliExpress

  - Suppliersdata

  - SaleHoo

  - Doba

- Wholesale2B

- Worldwide Brands

- Wholesale Central

- Sunrise Wholesale

- MegaGoods

- InventorySource

- National Dropshippers

- Dropshipper.com

- OfficeCrave.com

- ***Create your online store***

  Many platforms offer complete off-the-shelf eCommerce stores; my favorite is Shopify.com. It offers a full eCommerce platform with everything you will need to get up and running in a couple of hours. It is very easy to set up and design, even for the most basic of beginner levels, with a very low monthly cost of around $29. Shopify allows you to import products directly from various supplier sites, such as Aliexpress.com, using an add-on called Oberlo. It offers a complete order fulfillment process and payment gateways such as Paypal, as well as various SEO services to drive traffic to your site. It has an array of add-on platforms & apps that integrate seamlessly into the store for just about anything you need to run an eCommerce store. Below are my top 10 alternative platforms you can use to set up your eCommerce store, should you prefer not to use Shopify:

- Wix.com

- WooCommerce.com

- Yahoo Stores (Smallbusiness.yahoo.com)

- BigCommerce.com

- Volusion.com

- Shift4shop.com (3DCart)

- Magento.com

- Squarespace.com

- Salesforce Commerce Cloud (Salesforce.com/products/commerce-cloud)

- Yo-kart.com

- ***Start Selling***

It's as easy as 1-2-3! Now you have found your product(s) and set up your store, all that is left to do is start selling! Use Facebook Ads and/or Google Ads to get the word out and drive traffic and sales to your store! If you are not familiar with running ads, you can easily outsource this to a virtual assistant or a freelancer who specializes in ads that can run your campaigns for you. Set up social media accounts such as Instagram, TikTok, or Facebook to build your audience and market your products.

- **_Order fulfillment_**

  There is no better feeling than when that first sale comes in! Once you have made a sale, there are various ways you can fulfill orders. Assuming you are using Alexpress.com for your product supply, use the Oberlo add-on to manage the order fulfillment process. When an order comes in, with a few clicks of the button, Oberlo will place the order from the supplier on Aliexpress.com, who will, in turn, get the product sent out to your customer directly. When the order is placed with the supplier, they are advised in the Oberlo template not to include any of their own brandings so that the customer understands that they have purchased from you directly.

  It is also possible to make use of dropshipping agents to supply products and fulfill orders; they are generally used when you start to get a high level of orders each day.

Benefits of Dropshipping:

- No huge capital outlay or setup costs
- Quick and easy to get started, low barrier to entry
- Earn income from day one

- No need to hold or manage stock

- It can be run from anywhere with a laptop/smartphone and internet connection

- Capital required to start: $29+ for a Shopify store subscription

- Earning potential: Unlimited, $0 - $1m+ per month

- Time spent on business: 15 minutes per day

SUBSCRIPTIONS

"Ignoring online marketing is like opening a business but not telling anyone."

- Anonymous

What is a Subscription business model?

A subscription business model is an idea of selling a product or service by obtaining a commitment from your customers to place automated recurring orders and thereby creating regular ongoing subscription revenue. A customer would purchase a product or service and, whilst doing so, sign up for further regular orders that are generated automatically without the need for them to manually place each order. These can be monthly, bi-monthly, quarterly, 6 monthly, annually, etc.

Subscriptions emphasize the way revenue is generated so that a single customer pays multiple payments for prolonged access to goods or services. Subscriptions are a great strategy to implement into any of the business strategies you will learn in this book. It is a fantastic way to ensure automated repeat business.

Subscriptions these days are not limited to newspapers and magazines; they have taken on a whole new form of revenue production, which is implemented in many eCommerce stores. There are many things you could create subscriptions for in your business, the most common of which being subscription boxes, which could include an unlimited number of ideas such as various items of food and meal kits, treats and gifts, drinks and alcohol, pet treats and accessories (BarkBox), health and beauty products or makeup (Birchbox), regular household goods like paper towels and toilet paper, books and games, or Dollar Shave Club's recurring razor orders - the list is unlimited!

These are very easy to source from suppliers and can easily be implemented into your eCommerce store to be sold immediately.

As mentioned in our first lesson on Dropshipping, these

Steps to immediate passive income with Subscriptions:

- *Decide on your subscriptions business*

   Either add on a subscription model to your existing eCommerce or Dropshipping store by selecting any of your existing products that may be suitable to be sold on a subscription basis (basically any item a customer would want to purchase regularly). Options can be added to a particular product checkout page to either purchase as a once-off or as a subscription for a defined frequency giving your customers more choice. Alternatively, you could create an entirely new eCommerce store focussing solely on a particular subscription model, such as BarkBox's pet treats subscription box, which you could source from suppliers on sites such as Aliexpress.com and various other manufacturers.

Follow the steps mentioned in the Dropshipping module to market and sell your subscription products or services and fulfill orders.

Benefits of Subscriptions:

- The subscription pricing model attracts more customers; paying a lower monthly amount than a large lump sum is attractive.

- Recurring bill offers a predictable revenue stream, having a better idea of what your earnings will be

- Increased return on customer acquisition costs

- Capital required to start: $0, can simply be added to your existing store

- Earning potential: Unlimited

- Time spent on business: No additional time required; in fact, it will increase efficiency

AMAZON FBA (FULFILLED BY AMAZON)

"Success at the highest level comes down to one question: Can you decide that your happiness can come from someone else's success?"

- Bill Walton

They say that you should find a good mentor and learn from them. There is no better mentor when it comes to online business than the richest man in the world, Jeff Bezos, founder & CEO of Amazon. The key to passive income is setting up businesses that generate income and run themselves, and Jeff Bezos has created the ultimate solution for everyday people like ourselves to benefit from the massive success and growth Amazon has created. The FBA service provides full automation, which is exactly what we are looking for in our goal of $10,000 passive income per month.

Amazon FBA has undoubtedly become one of the most popular ways to earn a passive income online. In fact, over 2 million people are selling on Amazon worldwide, selling over 12 million products, with around 150 million customers who have Prime memberships. Prime customers spend, on average, around $1.4k

25

per year. In September 2019 alone, Amazon reached over 150.6 million mobile users who were accessing the Amazon application in that particular month! And Amazon FBA gives sellers a 30-50% increase in sales. Amazon brought in $125.6 Billion in sales revenue in the fourth quarter of 2020. It is evident that this is the place to be when it comes to creating passive income from selling online!

What is Amazon FBA?

This is probably best explained by Amazon themselves:

"Let Amazon pick, pack, and ship your orders. You sell it; we ship it... With Fulfillment by Amazon (FBA), you store your products in Amazon's fulfillment centers, and we pick, pack, ship, and provide customer service for these products. FBA can help you scale your business and reach more customers."

With Amazon FBA, the goal here is simple, find best-selling products to sell on Amazon, purchase the products from a supplier or manufacturer to be shipped to Amazon's warehouse, where they are stored for you. List your products on Amazon's website, where they are then sold, benefiting from their massive customer exposure, and Amazon will package and ship your products directly to the customer for each purchase. Amazon also takes care of all customer service inquiries, so you literally do not have to lift a finger! This is pure passive income automation at its finest, backed by a hugely successful company and their associated customer service team! Amazon charges a fee for their fulfillment service, which they deduct from the total sales revenue generated on their site before the balance is paid to your account, usually around every 14 days.

Case Study

Let's look at a basic example of selling an iPhone cover on Amazon FBA to put things into perspective, using an Amazon seller as an example: a brand called SURPHY.

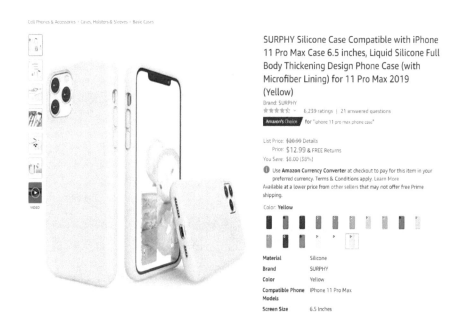

With a very quick search on Alibaba.com, I found a great-looking silicone iPhone cover from a manufacturer with fast shipping to the U.S.; they have a minimum order quantity of 50 units without any customizations being made to the product.

50 Pieces   **US$12.50**

Ship to United States
by Alibaba.com Air ...   **US$27.38**

Lead Time **5** days ⓘ

Shipping time **5-9** days ⓘ

Total   **US$39.88**

Start Order

✉Contact Supplier

📞 Call us

🛒 Add to cart

◎**Gold Supplier**

Now belongs to your color

Ready to Ship   ⊘ In Stock ⊘ Fast Dispa

2021 Wholesale Shockproof TPU (
Max Hot sale products

★ ★ ★ ★ ★ 5.0 2 Reviews   17 buye

50 - 999 Pieces   1000 - 4999 Pie
$0.25   **$0.21**

MARCH EXPO   · Free shipping (up to US

Color:

Material: TPU

Bundle: 1 phone 11

                  1 phone 11 pro

ⓘ View larger image

28

Check out the numbers:

- **$0.25** - Cost price per unit x 50 units = **$12.50** Total Cost of Goods (COG)

- **$27.38** - Shipping fee to U.S. Amazon warehouse (5-9 days delivery)

- **$39.88** - Total order amount ($12.50 COG + $27.38 shipping)

- **$0.80** - Landed Cost per iPhone cover delivered to Amazon's warehouse (rounded off)

- **$12.99** - Sale price per unit on Amazon.com for the identical iPhone case

- **$4.95** - Fees deducted by Amazon for each sale

- **$7.24** - Profit per unit sold (55.74% Margin)

- **$362** - Total Profit on 50 units

You can use the Amazon FBA Revenue Calculator tool to calculate estimated revenue and fees using a competitor's ASIN (product number). The below calculator can be found by searching 'Amazon FBA Revenue Calculator' in Google.

Amazon Fulfillment

Revenue

Item price	$	12.99
Shipping	$	0.00
Total revenue	$	12.99
Selling on Amazon fees	$	1.95 ˅

Fulfillment cost

Cost of seller fulfillment		N/A
Fulfillment by Amazon fees	$	2.50 ˅
Ship to Amazon	$	0.00
Total fulfillment cost	$	2.50

Storage cost

Monthly storage cost per unit	$	0.01
Average inventory units stored		50
Storage cost per unit sold	$	0.50

Seller proceeds	$	8.04
Cost of product	$	0.80

Net profitability

Net profit	$	7.24
Net margin		55.74%

LQS:	7	#1869 in Cell Phones & Accessories
Mo. Sales:	2,707	#411 in Cell Phone Basic Cases
Net:	$8.54	
Fees:	$4.45	
Date First Available:	07/18/2020	
Tier:	Standard (Small)	
Dimensions:	5.0" x 8.3" x 0.5"	
Weight:	0.06lbs	

At the time of publishing, using the earlier tool I mentioned (Junglescout.com, as pictured above), I identified that the particular seller used in my example is selling around 2707 units of this particular iPhone case on Amazon.com on average each month. Therefore, if you were selling the same numbers as this seller, this would equate to a monthly profit of **$19,598.68!!**

Almost double our $10,000 per month goal on just one product!

I bet you never thought you could make this much just on an iPhone case! There are many profitable products out there; the earning potential is unlimited.

Steps to immediate passive income with Amazon FBA:

- *Source best selling products*

There are numerous methods of sourcing best-selling products. I have found that the best way in which to do so is through proven analytical data collected from Amazon. There are various tools that can be used to determine which products are selling well and which are most profitable with the lowest amount of competition (reviews). I have used Jungelscout.com and Helium10.com, which both offer excellent tools to analyze all the data that is available on Amazon. These tools are paid for; however, they are well worth the money; in my opinion, as product selection is one of the most important aspects of being successful on Amazon, it is extremely important you select the right products with proven sales volume, and these tools and the resources they provide on how to use them are extremely useful in this process. It is also possible to analyze data without these tools for free, but it is more time-consuming. An entire book can be dedicated exclusively to product research and FBA as a whole, but I aim to provide a basic outline to get you started in the right direction. Most products can be sourced from one of the largest wholesale manufacturer online directories, Alibaba.com. Manufacturers and suppliers on this site are based all over the world; there is not much you can't find on Alibaba.com.

- ***Private Labelling or Reselling?***

Private labeling is my preferred method of selling on Amazon when it comes to product selection/creation, as this allows you to source a product to sell but to create your own brand around that product setting you apart from other products and sellers, making yours more desirable, generating more sales. In a nutshell, private labeling is when a product is manufactured by one company (the manufacturer or supplier) which is then branded for, marketed, and sold by another company (you). This allows you to choose your own brand name, create and design your own product packaging, logo and even customize the product features, size, finishes, etc. - a fully customizable product that you create to make your own according to the needs of your customers based on your customer research. Checking negative customer reviews of competitor products will hint at changes you could make to improve the product, making yours superior. Most elements within this product creation process can easily be outsourced to freelancers, such as log and packaging design, listing images and infographics, etc. There will usually be larger minimum order quantities for customized products which will increase your initial capital outlay. Factor in any graphic design costs, which are usually quite cheap, e.g., you can get a customized package design on Fiverr.com for as little as $5. You can also purchase products as they are, without customizing them but still sell them as your brand. The minimum order quantities in these instances are lower and therefore require lower capital outlay and lower graphic design costs.

Alternatively, you could source and resell existing branded products; however, I would not recommend this route as the margins are low, and this involves more work. There are loads of restrictions on which can and can't be resold, not to mention the high competition with other big brand stores where these brands are already established, making it a lot more difficult to stand out amongst the crowd.

- ***Buy stock and ship to Amazon.***

Once you have sourced your products, negotiated and agreed quantities and prices, you are now ready to purchase the wholesale stock and get them shipped to an Amazon warehouse. Many manufacturers found on Alibaba.com offer shipping services direct to Amazon FBA warehouses; alternatively, you can find a freight forwarder who is an agent who specializes in shipping wholesale stock internationally that can handle everything for you. My suggestion would be to use a freight forwarder as they can offer a complete service and take care of all the shipping for you. The shipping process, terminology, charges, and taxes can be slightly confusing to some who have never dealt with this before, and a freight forwarder can ensure that you don't need to concern yourself with the details. Remember, the aim is to make use of the resources around us to be as efficient as possible, even if it means it costs a little more, as we want to achieve a passive income which means minimal input from ourselves.

- *Sit back, relax and watch the money roll in!*

Amazon will receive your stock and get it organized in their warehouse, ready to be picked and shipped to their customers each time you get a sale. You will need an Amazon seller/merchant account, so you can create your product listing on their website, which will include product images (which can often be obtained from your suppliers), descriptions, and associated product keywords that customers would search to find your product. Once you publish your Amazon listing to the site for customers to start buying, you can rest assured that the hard work is now over. Moving forward, Amazon will take care of the rest, ensuring products are sent to their customers when purchased, and these will be sent via Prime Delivery, where customers have a Prime membership. They will handle any customer queries directly, and you will be paid fortnightly for all the sales generated, minus Amazon fees. You won't necessarily need to spend any time on the business once your listing is published and your stock is in the warehouse; you may want to spend some time checking and responding to customer reviews to ensure your customers are happy or to drive further sales through advertising (Amazon PPC).

- **_Restock/replenish when you sell out_**

  Very soon, you will sell out, and you will need to replenish your stock. I always try to ensure at least 6 months' worth of stock is available at the Amazon warehouse when I place orders from my suppliers; however, if you can find suppliers with reliable, fast shipping times, then you can reduce the amount of stock held by Amazon and thereby reduce Amazon storage fees. When it comes time to reorder, simply message your supplier or manufacturer advising of the quantity you require, arrange the payment to your supplier for the stock, and arrange to ship to Amazon's warehouse. Then that is your work done until the next time you need to replenish again. Easy! If you do this once every 6 months, you will only spend a couple of hours per year on this business!

Benefits of Amazon FBA:

- The one business where you don't have to sell, Amazon brings the sales to you!

- Amazon takes care of warehousing stock, picking, packing, shipping & customer service - the complete package.

- When Amazon grows, you grow.

- Capital required to start: As little as $39+ depending on the stock purchased, as demonstrated in the above example

- Earning potential: Unlimited, $0 - $500k+ per month

- Time spent on business: 5-10 Minutes per day

PRINT ON DEMAND

"Creativity doesn't wait for that perfect moment. It fashions its own perfect moments out of ordinary ones."

- Bruce Garrabrandt

Print on demand is another form of Dropshipping but is perhaps considered the more creative as this is where you can let your creative juices flow to come up with amazing personalized products. Customized items are in very high demand; customers love to be unique and stand out from the crowds!

What is Print on Demand?

Print on demand is when you sell your custom designs on your eCommerce store, either designed yourself or obtained from other sources, which are printed on various products of your choice such as T-Shirts and apparel, face masks, mugs, phone cases, pet products, stationery and office equipment, puzzles, homeware, tech accessories and so, so much more! In the same case as Dropshipping, the supplier ships the products directly to your customers on your behalf.

Setting up, again, is very easy. You will create an eCommerce store and then integrate a Print on Demand service (supplier) into your store. When your customer makes a purchase of whichever unique products you decide to sell, the order will integrate with the supplier, who will print the item, package it, and ship it to your customer for you.

There are loads of awesome Print on Demand suppliers that you can choose from who seamlessly integrate with eCommerce platforms such as Shopify. See below for a list of suppliers I can recommend checking out:

- Printful.com

- Zazzle.com

- Redbubble.com

- TeeSpring.com

- CustomCat.com

- Printify.com

- Printaura.com

- Teelaunch.com

- Viralstyle.com

- Society6.com

Case Study

Mooshe Socks (Shopmooshesocks.com) is a vibrant dropshipping company selling socks that come in all sorts of cool designs and colors. When looking at their store, you would never think that they are actually a print-on-demand dropshipping store. They have also incorporated a Subscription service model, like the one we covered in an earlier module, boosting their regular revenue from customers wanting a regular supply of socks. This is a great example of a fun store that can easily be set up as a successful print-on-demand business.

Steps to immediate passive income with Print on Demand:

- **Source best selling products**

  Have an idea of your own or something you would like to design? Great, now is the time to realize that dream! Not have anything in mind? No problem, browse the product ranges from the print-on-demand suppliers listed above and see which products catch your eye. Try to find something that is unique and creative, that will stand out, and which you can create a great-looking store around. Use Google Trends to see which search terms/products are trending. Browse the best sellers of popular websites such as Amazon.com, Etsy, etc., for inspiration.

- **Create your store and brand**

  If you already have a store, then great, you can skip this step. If you don't already have a store, much like we have done in earlier modules, you can set up a store easily with Shopify.com. Create and design your store around a catchy brand that aligns with the products you are selling and the message you want to put across. Remember, feel free to make use of freelancers wherever necessary to reduce the amount of time you spend on tedious tasks or on those where skills may be slightly lacking.

- **Team up with your Print on Demand supplier**

  Many of the above-listed suppliers will integrate seamlessly with a Shopify store. Do your research on how much you will sell your products for, which countries you intend to sell to, how much it will cost to supply your print-on-demand products from your supplier, and what their shipping times are to your customers. Set up the integration, then you are good to go! Most eCommerce platforms and suppliers will have step-by-step guides on how to integrate into your store.

- **Get creative**

This is where the fun kicks in! Come up with your design ideas of what you want to print on your products. Try to be unique and current, getting ahead of the trends. You can create your own designs yourself if you choose to. Maybe you are already a skilled designer with access to high-tech software such as Adobe, or maybe you are a complete beginner with a passion for succeeding. There is no need for you to go out and buy any expensive software; there are loads of free platforms out there with various templates you can edit to your taste. I often use Canva.com, a free web-based platform with loads of designs and templates you can easily edit yourself.

No desire to do the work yourself? No problem; working smarter rather than harder is the name of the game! Outsource the design on Fiverr.com or Upwork.com for as little as $5! Some Print on Demand stores also offers their own design templates you can use and customize.

- **Start selling & fulfill orders!**

In exactly the same way you learned about how to market and sell in the earlier Dropshipping module, replicate those strategies to market, sell and fulfill product orders. Get the word out there about your awesome products, and you have done it again, adding another passive income revenue stream to the $10,000 per month goal!

Benefits of Print on Demand:

- Get creative and have some fun with your business

- No huge capital outlay or setup costs

- Quick and easy to get started, low barrier to entry

- Earn income from day one

- No need to hold or manage stock

- It can be run from anywhere with a laptop/smartphone and internet connection.

- Capital required to start: $29+ for a Shopify store subscription

- Earning potential: Unlimited, $0 - $500k+ per month

- Time spent on business: 10-15 minutes per day

AFFILIATE MARKETING

"To have an impact on your audience, you must understand their pain points."

- Neil Patel

What is Affiliate Marketing?

Very simply put, this is the system of earning commission through promoting other people or companies' products. You find other people's products, which usually align with your existing business or audience, promote them and earn a share of the profit for each sale made through your referral link. This is an online sales tactic letting product owners increase their revenue by letting others (you) who are targeting a similar audience - "affiliates" - earn commission from product recommendations whilst simultaneously making it possible for affiliates to earn additional revenue on product sales without having to actually create products of their own.

But why would you want to promote other people's products, you ask? Very often, your business aligns with other complementary products within your niche that you have no interest in selling or creating yourself but which will be of benefit to your customers or following. Considering you share a similar customer base and you are already promoting your products or services to your customer base, you can also mention complimentary products to your customer base, which may not be in direct competition with you. If your customers make a purchase using the referral link or discount code you share with them, then the merchant (who owns the product you are recommending) will pay you a pre-agreed commission. Affiliate marketing is a great way to earn an additional revenue stream off the back of your existing business or even as a standalone entity promoting lots of products, such as a blog or podcast.

Case Study

A hypothetical example of this would be someone who has their own cooking channel on Youtube; let's make up a name and call them 'Chef Luigi.' Chef Luigi may post video and content on his channel or online blogs and website promoting his recipes and cookbooks for sale to his customer base. Chef Luigi only sells cookbooks and has no interest in selling any other products, however during his cooking process, he often uses impressive products, let's say, for instance, a great food processor from a company we will name 'Kitchen Lover,' which Chef Luigi really likes because it gets the job done well. Chef Luigi agrees to an affiliate partnership with the seller of the food processor (Kitchen Lover), whereby Chef Luigi will receive a percentage of the sale price of any sale generated from his referral link or discount code which he shares with his customer base in his usual promotions for his own cookbooks. 45

Some other examples of great affiliate program products include fashion & apparel, computer products and accessories, health and wellbeing products, vehicle and bicycle accessories, and loads more.

Steps to immediate passive income with Affiliate Marketing:

- *Find and join an affiliate program*

  It's time to dive in and find the affiliate programs best suited for your business. Again, there are so many to choose from. There are affiliate networks that you can join, offering a selection of brands and offers to work with, whilst some companies manage their own affiliate program in-house. The quickest and easiest way to get started would be to have a look at an affiliate marketplace where you can browse your chosen niche to find top-performing affiliate platforms to partner with. Below are some popular platforms to get you started:

  - Avantlink.com

  - Clickbank.com

  - Affiliatefuture.com

  - Linkconnector.com

  - Cj.com

  - Revenuewire.com

- Flexoffers.com

- Shareasale.com

- ***Choose offers you wish to promote***
  Whilst browsing through the different options available, the most important factor to keep in consideration is your niche. It is imperative that you select offers that align with your existing niche or your existing customer base or following. The idea is that you don't want to put extra energy into marketing to people outside of your existing audience, as this will add additional time and expense. If you don't already have an existing audience, then that is fine; you will build an audience but try to ensure you are building an audience who share common interests, ensuring they will see value in the products you will recommend. For instance, a food blogger wouldn't promote beauty products. But they may promote a wide range of other products which would fit within their niche, such as cookware, recipes, cookbooks, meal kits, etc. Once you have selected your offers, obtain your unique affiliate link for each offer that you will use to promote. In order to be paid a commission, the purchase must be made through your audience clicking that particular link so that the sale is associated with your account.

- ***Spread the word; it's all about marketing.***

  Now it's time to get the word out; sharing is caring! Share the affiliate links to your customer audience using various strategies. You can create blogs to provide value to your audience, run social media campaigns on Instagram and Facebook. Setup email marketing campaigns or include the links in your existing email marketing campaigns to your customer audience. Offering promotions, discount codes, or coupons are another great way to get customers to buy. You could also create helpful content, such as how-to videos, to overcome your audience's everyday problems through product video demos. You could also add advertising banners, buttons, and links to various parts of your website or blogs.

- ***Get paid***

  Collect a commission each time someone uses your link to complete a purchase. Commission rates vary considerably depending on the company and the offer. The lower end of the spectrum will earn you around 5% of the sale; however, with some affiliate arrangements, you can earn as high as 50%, usually when promoting something such as a class or event. Some affiliate marketing programs pay a fixed fee flat rate as opposed to a commission percentage.

Benefits of Affiliate Marketing:

- Very easy to do, no product creation, marketing is the only element

- No capital outlay is required at all

- Very low risk, there is no cost or regular expenses involved

- Earn an income instantly

- Allows you to scale your business revenue without hiring additional help

- It can be run from anywhere with a laptop/smartphone and internet connection

- Capital required to start: $0

- Earning potential: Unlimited, $0 - $200k+ per month

- Time spent on business: 5 minutes per day

ONLINE COURSES

"An investment in knowledge pays the best interest. "

- Benjamin Franklin

The time to build and sell online courses is now! Education is in constant demand, provides excellent value to its consumers, and in today's world, the content to build the course is often free or inexpensive to come by, which translates to excellent profit margins. Millions of people are purchasing online courses, both inside and outside of the traditional educational system, to upgrade their knowledge or skills on every manner of topics. They prefer a step-by-step, clearly laid out and organized course, which provides support, as opposed to spending hours navigating the free information minefield online, which often sends them down numerous rabbit holes for hours - in the end, learning little, ending up only with more confusion. You can create and sell courses on topics such as social media marketing, building websites, cell phone repairs, business & entrepreneurship, arts & crafts, health & fitness, education, and personal development; the options are endless!

What are Online Courses?

A pretty self-explanatory term everyone is likely to already be aware of, online courses are an alternative to studying at a school or college. Instead of attending lectures and seminars, you learn from the comfort of your own home or wherever you choose. All teaching materials are delivered online, and you can learn at your own pace whenever you choose to do so.

How much can you make? Online courses are extremely profitable; you can earn anywhere from $0 - $50,000+ per month as a starter, sometimes even up to $1m+ per month, depending on the course and level of expertise or quality of content you can offer. There are many factors that may affect your income potential, such as the sale price of your course, the size of the niche, and the size of the audience you are marketing to. Your goal is to provide as much high-quality, value content surrounding a particular topic as possible in an organized and easy-to-understand manner.

Case Study

There is no better success story when it comes to online courses than the one featured on Forbes.com about Joseph Michael, a regular dad from Missouri who achieved fantastic success in a journey to earn over $100,000 per year through online courses. Living from paycheck to paycheck, he created an online course to help others to learn to use a tricky writing software platform to boost their writing careers. He has created online courses to help fledgling writers and entrepreneurs achieve their dreams.

Joseph started with a blog called Efficient Life Skills, targeted towards helping people learn how to do things faster. Inspired by a shoe-tying lesson his daughter learned in 5 minutes, he went on to create a step-by-step video that people could use to teach their own kids how to tie their shoes. The video went viral and has since had 800,000 shares; this eventually led to him creating an online course relating to a word processing program and earning a passive income from it through educating people based on research of his own, with no experience of online courses at all!

Steps to immediate passive income with Online Courses:

- *Decide what you would like to teach*

  Online courses tie in very well where businesses or individuals have existing followings; for instance, a chef selling cookbooks could offer their customers access to an online course where pre-recorded videos teach advanced cooking techniques, skills, and recipes. Alternatively, you could also set up an online course from scratch even if you don't have an existing following or audience, but you would then need to build an audience through marketing to promote the course to. Look at you're existing or planned business ventures and deduce if an online course could be introduced; this is usually the easiest way to decide what to teach. Alternatively, draw upon your professional or life experiences to find something you are passionate about teaching and go from there. You could also search online for the most popular online courses currently being sold and see which you would be most passionate about. Passion is important when selecting any product or service to sell or promote, as it is easier to remain motivated about something you are passionate about.

A great little exercise you can do to get started is simply to make a list of 10-20 of your passions or interests, alongside that list your skills, experience, and achievements within each of those interests, and then choose the ones which intersect the most, and which you feel most passionate about. Ask yourself, which of these could I talk about for ages without becoming bored? You will be surprised at how quickly you will find a great idea.

- *Identify your customer and validate demand.*

Work out who the course will appeal to so that you can identify your target audience, and remember just because it appeals to you does not necessarily mean that it will appeal to everyone. If you try to create a course that will appeal to everyone, it is likely to appeal to no one. Niche down as much as possible to find a specific target market which will then be easier to market to. If you have an existing customer base, then find out exactly who they are and what appeals to them. Validate the demand for your course by researching your competition, find other people or companies who are offering the same or similar courses or who serve the same target audience. Check out best-selling Amazon books, other online courses from a Google search, 'gurus' who have a following on Youtube, podcasts, etc. If other people are successfully selling online courses on the same topic, then this is a good sign; however, if you cannot find any other courses on the same topic, this could be a red flag that there may be no demand. Another way to validate demand, if you have an existing target audience, is to simply ask them what they want to learn. This can be done via email marketing and surveys as well as on social media posts encouraging them to comment on topics.

- ***Create the course***

  Let the fun begin! This is one of the more exciting steps, but it can be time-consuming, so try to be as efficient and as organized as possible. Identify exactly what you want your students to take away and learn from the course, and then map out exactly how you will deliver this to them.

  - Start with your topic title.

  - Create a course outline, lesson by lesson

- Create or record your content. You can choose to create text, audio, or video content - most courses include all of these. I find video content to be the best way of communicating a lesson online. You can record content yourself free of charge using your smartphone; you don't need any high-tech equipment for this. Alternatively, outsource this to a freelancer if you prefer

- Set up your course website or platform. Whilst not originally set up to accommodate online courses, if you already have a Shopify website set up, you can use Shopify.com along with an add-on from the Shopify App Store. Thinkific is an app you could use; however, there are many different apps available to choose from. Kajabi.com is a popular platform to create courses that work really well and offers a mobile application that is very handy to your students learning on the go!

- Create a members-only Facebook group for your course. This will allow you to easily interact with your students but also provides a platform for students to interact with each other where they can provide value and support to one another, therefore requiring less input from you

- Test the course content and usability from a student's perspective before going live

- *Get the word out*

  Once your course is ready, it is time to let the world know about it! Decide on a pricing model that works for you, do your research to see what competitor courses are selling for. You can create offers and discounts to instill urgency to purchase. Focus on customer success to promote your course. People want to know that they will successfully achieve the desired outcome once they have completed your course. You can market it in the usual methods already covered in previous modules via social media campaigns, paid advertising campaigns, email marketing, etc.

- *Provide support*

  Students will likely have questions they need answering; a great way to deal with this is by setting up a FAQ section on your website where they can find answers to commonly asked questions. You can also direct them to the Facebook community, where other accomplished members are able to answer their questions without the need for you to get involved. You can also provide value to your students by offering a regular Q&A webinar, where their questions can be answered in one sitting, for instance, once a month. Once your member numbers grow, you want to ensure that you are not getting too involved in the business so that you can ensure the income is passive and you do not fall back to becoming an employee rather than a business owner. There are various methods you could adopt in providing support without needing to be directly involved in this yourself. You could elect mentors from your student pool who have demonstrated success through their achievements in the course and offer them remuneration for hosting the regular Q&A's or assigning a Facebook group moderator who answers any questions students may have. These tasks can also be outsourced to freelancers with experience or knowledge in your chosen topic.

Benefits of Online Courses:

- Easy-to-use platforms simplify the course-creation process

- You can offer courses that complement your existing business

- Create passive income by reselling the same course continually

- You can use an online course to lead customers to other product offers & vice versa

- Online availability means you can target customers worldwide

- Capital required to start: $0

- Earning potential: Unlimited, most earn $0 - $50,000+ per month but can go as high as $1m+

- Time spent on business: 30 minutes per day

REAL ESTATE CROWDFUNDING

"Ninety percent of all millionaires become so through owning real estate."

- Andrew Carnegie

Ever wanted to invest in real estate but never had the capital, know-how, or time to do so? Then crowdfunding is a great way to begin. I'm sure you have already heard the term 'crowdfunding' before; perhaps you have invested in crowdfunding projects or even obtained investment financing from crowdfunding platforms for your own projects. Crowdfunding can serve many purposes; it is a great starting point to get into the real estate game. For the purposes of this lesson, we will make use of crowdfunding as a way to invest in real estate without having to fork out loads of cash and by minimizing our risk to some degree. It is a lower barrier to entry form of real estate investment, where someone else does all the legwork for us.

What is Crowdfunding?

Crowdfunding is a way of pooling money together from a group of investors in order to make an investment into a project, company, or business, usually requiring a large amount of capital. It relies upon the power of many, with smaller capital investments, to achieve a larger goal or outcome that would have been more difficult to achieve on your own. Crowdfunding lets small-time investors fund large projects.

The first incidence of modern crowdfunding was in 1997 when a British rock band called Marillion raised money from their fans to fund their U.S. tour. While crowdfunding is a relatively new term when comparing it to other, more traditional investment strategies, the core element of its function has, in fact, existed for centuries. Friends, family, partners, and institutions have come together to purchase property collectively for many years. The main difference between collective real estate investing of the past and crowdfunding for real estate today; is the ability to transact online by a much wider, global audience, using the internet as a new distribution platform that brings together a greater collective buying power.

Given the advances of modern technology in today's world, investors no longer need to go out beating the streets and knocking on doors to find great investment deals. Instead, investors can now find and browse deals online from the comfort of their homes, sign legal agreements securely online, transfer funds, and gain access to investor dashboards to manage their investments and see how they are performing in real-time. No need to exhaustively carry out due diligence on hundreds of potential projects to find the one that is right to invest in, only to later realize you missed something detrimental. With crowdfunding, investors can browse pre-qualified, pre-curated investments through crowdfunding platforms, which have teams of in-house experts analyzing all the data, crunching the numbers, doing the hard work for you.

The types of investments you can make.

Generally, there are two main types of investments you can make when using real estate crowdfunding:

1. Equity Investments

Equity investments are like owning shares in an apartment building. This type of investment will return a share in the cash flow of the project from rents on a regular ongoing basis and appreciation in value when the property is sold. Much like when you purchase a property yourself, you will outlay a large sum of cash to purchase the property; when you rent it out, you will get a monthly rental income, and then when you sell it, you will make a profit on the capital appreciation it has gained over time. The equity investment model scales this down to an investment level that you can afford. Rather than requiring a large capital outlay upfront, you can invest at a level that is affordable to you whilst getting the same benefits in proportion to your initial investment. I have seen some crowdfunding platforms offering investment levels from as little as $100, but most will usually start a little higher at around $500 minimum investment.

2. Secured Loans

In this strategy, you are essentially acting as the bank in the real-life game of monopoly. Your investment is treated as a loan, similar to a bank making a loan, which is secured against the real estate project. These loans pay you a monthly interest, often a lot higher than any interest-bearing account you would get from a bank, and the investment is secured by the property, so it is relatively low risk.

The main difference between the two investment types above is that the equity investment strategy allows you to share in the upside in property value and in the cash flow from rents which usually change slightly in value from tenancy to tenancy dependant on the market (and are usually paid quarterly); whereas loans allow the investor to receive a consistent, monthly income stream with less volatility as this will be at a fixed rate.

"Roughly 90% of millionaires—yes, 9 out of 10—created their wealth through real estate," says Kurt M. Westfield, managing partner of W.C. Companies in Tampa, Florida. "Not stocks. Not gold. Not baseball cards or other seasonal or whimsical investment vehicles."

How much can I make from real estate crowdfunding?

What you earn will be dependent on your level of investment and the length of time you choose to invest. Typically you can achieve around 12% annual return on your investment; however, this can swing higher or lower year-to-year. Like with traditional real estate investing, it is not without risks; property values can increase as well as decrease; however, being a crowdfunding investor definitely limits your risk.

When investing in rental properties as an owner rather than as a crowdfunding investor, an owner is faced with all the hassles and hardships that come with property: nagging tenants, late-night emergency property maintenance, calls at all hours over minuscule issues, etc. The beauty of crowdfunding investment is that you don't need to deal with all this hassle; your investment is a truly passive one. This is a fantastic passive income stream to add to your arsenal to achieve your $10,000+ per month goal.

Steps to immediate passive income with Real Estate Crowdfunding:

- *Choose a crowdfunding platform*

  There are many different types of platforms to choose from, often, you will need to register to browse the deals on offer, and you may need to be vetted for security purposes.

- Fundrise.com   (Invest $500+)

- Diversyfund.com   (Invest $500+)

- Crowdstreet.com   (Invest $1,000+)

- Peerstreet.com   (Invest $1,000+)

- Realtymogul.com   (Invest $5,000+)

- Patchofland.com   (Invest $5,000+)

- Prodigynetwork.com   (Invest $10,000+)

- Realcrowd.com   (Invest $25,000+)

- ***Find a deal & invest.***

Decide on the level of investment you are comfortable making; how much can you afford to put in? Your funds will usually be tied in for a certain period of time; find out the minimum term required as well as what your options are for pulling the funds out. The more funds you invest, the higher the level of passive income that you will earn, but only invest what you are comfortable with. Decide on the investment type, whether you prefer a 'share' (equity investment) or you simply want to make a 'loan' (secured loans). Browse the different investment deals available at the time, analyzing, in particular, the level of investment required and the return being offered. Go over all the details to fully understand the deal, and reach out to the crowdfunding platform if you have any questions at all. Pick a deal and pull the trigger.

- **_Watch the money roll in_**

  Depending on the deal you have selected, there will be different ways and frequencies in which you will earn your returns. The crowdfunding platform will make it very clear how and when your returns will be paid. You will usually gain access to an online dashboard that you can log in to at any time and see how your investments are doing. Once you have made your investment, there is no further time required to be spent on the business. It is truly passive. You can, however, choose to reinvest your earnings or put further funds into other projects in order to build your portfolio.

Benefits of Real Estate Crowdfunding:

- Higher returns than other investments

- Small initial investment

- Lower risk than traditional real estate investing

- Easily diversify your portfolio by investing in many properties' types

- Get to invest in real estate, but without the associated headache tenants bring

- Capital required to start: $500+

- Earning potential: Around 12% annual return on average, based on capital invested

- Time spent on business: 0 minutes per day

eTORO COPY TRADING

"If you want to be successful, find someone who has achieved the results you want and copy what they do and you'll achieve the same results."

- Tony Robbins

Have you wanted to invest in stocks, shares, or cryptocurrencies but either lack the knowledge, ability, or motivation to do so on your own accord? Investing in stocks, shares, and crypto requires a lot of research, dedication, and hard work. Unless you are already knowledgeable or have experience within this field, it can seem like a very confusing place for the everyday person. You have to have the skills to analyze the performance and numbers of often very large corporations, try to figure out for yourself how they will perform in the future, and then invest your hard-earned cash based on your limited knowledge and research. For a beginner in the world of stocks and shares, this can seem very daunting and can be extremely risky, ending up in financial losses and extremely stressful situations.

eToro is a platform that makes it much easier for the everyday person and experienced investors alike; to invest in stocks, shares, and cryptocurrencies but with the backing of more knowledgeable and experienced investors and traders.

What is eToro Copy Trading?

eToro is the pioneer when it comes to this relatively new concept of Copy Trading, which was born out of Mirror Trading. Copy Trading empowers you to automatically copy other traders (Popular Investors) of your choice, replicating their trades in your own accounts. To put it plainly, it is a means to trade in the financial markets by utilizing other traders from around the globe to do the trading on your behalf.

eToro incorporates a social element into its platform, whereby you can see exactly what other traders are doing in real-time. You can communicate with, follow and copy the top-performing traders so that you can realize the same gains as them. eToro has a patented copy trading technology; it is a tool that allows you to automatically copy other successful traders, opening the same positions as them in real-time. You find successful traders on the platform to copy by analyzing their trading statistics shown on their profiles, invest some funds into the account, and then benefit from the gains they make as you are essentially replicating their trades, benefiting from their invaluable experience and expertise. With eToro, you are essentially building a portfolio of successful people. This is the perfect platform for someone who does not have the time or devotion to learn the in-depth world of the financial markets.

It is worth noting, as with any investment, that you can realize some fantastic gains, but you can also realize losses, so it is not without risk.

However, eToro assigns a risk score rating between 1-10 to each member profile which helps investors assess the level of risk they are taking. A risk score of 1 is very low, whilst a score of 10 is high. The risk score is calculated using a unique algorithm developed by eToro and is based on the trader's past performance and behavior in terms of their choice of instruments, leverage, percentage of equity invested, etc. When combining all the data, eToro is able to calculate, with a high degree of accuracy, the risk a trader brings to your portfolio.

How do I make money?

eToro lets you, as the copy trader, copy other Popular Investors (traders). The amount you earn is dependent on the capital you invest and how much of that capital you allocate to each Popular Investor. When you copy a Popular Investor, you get a percentage of the profit that the investor made off the money invested. For example, if you invested $200 with an investor, and their gain on their trades was 30%, then you will receive $60 in profit. If you invested $1000, then your profit would be $300. As per eToro's statistics shown below, the 50 most copied traders for 2020 on eToro had an average yearly profit of 83.7%. This equates to a profit of $837 on only $1000 invested!

'eToro'

When they trade, you trade

Whether you're a beginner learning the basics or you simply don't have time to watch the markets, now it's easy to leverage other traders' expertise. With eToro's CopyTrader, you can automatically copy top-performing traders, instantly replicating their trading in your own portfolio.

AVERAGE YEARLY PROFIT

83.7% ↑

of our 50 most copied traders for 2020

Another way to earn money is by becoming a Popular Investor on eToro, where other members copy your trades. You will, however, need to have extensive experience or exceptional trade performance and meet certain criteria set by eToro to become a Popular Investor. eToro has different levels of Popular Investor structures paying various amounts and percentages based on the performance of your trades. This is considered a highly advanced level, but one which you could advance to at a later stage.

Case Study

Let's take a look at an elite-status Popular Investor I follow on eToro called Harry Stephen Harrison (eToro username: *HarryH1993*). Harry originally joined eToro to invest his own money and later discovered, through being a Popular Investor, that he could earn an income for others as well as himself. He is based in the U.K. and is now a full-time Popular Investor. His strategy is focussed mainly on technology and energy stocks, with a target to hold all investments for 3 years+. He suggests a copy amount of around $500, but of course, a higher investment will mean larger returns. He had 16,847 followers and 3,686 copiers at the time of publishing. Looking at Harry's stats is where it gets really exciting. See the below image; in 2019, he realized a gain of **43.47%,** and then in 2020, a massive gain of **115.89%.** If you had invested only $1000 at the start of 2019, then you would have earned a profit of **$434.70** in that year, and in 2020 you would have earned another **$1,158.90.** Not taking into account the complexities of the compounding effect in our calculations, simply put, this equates to a profit of **$1593.60** from an initial $1000 investment, essentially turning your $1000 into **$2,593.60** total.

Think about how much you would have earned if investing $5000 or $10,000!

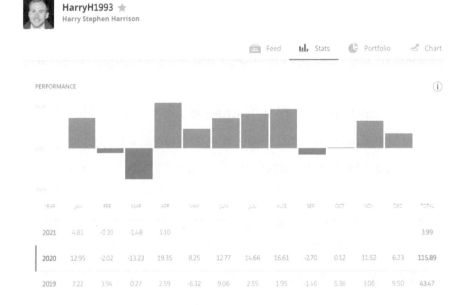

Steps to immediate passive income with eToro Copy Trading:

- *Create an eToro account*

  Creating an account is very easy; simply go to eToro.com. Click 'Join Now' and follow the prompts on the screen. There are no management fees or hidden charges to pay.

- *Find top-performing traders to copy*

  Your best bet is to start with the most Popular Investors in the Editor's Choice section in the 'Copy People' tab. Highlighted here will be traders who have shown gains in recent months and have maintained low-risk scores. Next, you can make use of the people discovery tool, where you can find more traders to copy. The search results can be easily filtered based on your preferences on risk score, level of gains, country of origin, and various other factors. eToro has numerous lists of top performers, including categories such as 'most copied,' 'trending,' and different strategy types. Click on their profiles to do your research, read their profiles and posts on their feed, check on their stats for current and previous periods to see what level of gains or losses they have made, check their risk scores to ensure you are matching with a level you are comfortable with and have a look at their portfolio and their charts to review performance further. Be mindful that past performance does not necessarily mean the same performance will be replicated in the future, but it does recognize the fact that if they have had continued success in the past, they are likely to know what they are doing. Some traders will have a minimum copy amount displayed on their profile; it is advisable to ensure you match that minimum to achieve the best results, as you may not achieve the same gains shown in their statistics if you invest less than their proposed minimum. Traders also often advise on a timescale in which they recommend you invest for, in order to maximize gains based on the specific strategy that the trader adopts within their portfolio. In saying this, though, you can withdraw your funds at any time you choose; there is no tie-in period. Add the people who interest you to your watchlist to revise later.

- ***Time to copy top performers & earn!***

Having narrowed down the traders you are interested in copying, review their stats again from your watchlist and decide on who you want to copy and what level of initial investment you want to start at. It may be good to start with 1-3 traders. You can invest from as little as $200. Deposit funds into your eToro account to begin copying. Select the trader profile, click copy, enter the amount you wish to allocate. Ensure 'Copy Open Trades' is ticked, then click copy. You will be duplicating their positions in real-time, automatically, and in direct proportion. Once you have copied a trader, then that is it; you will simply log in occasionally to see how your portfolio is doing. When you click on your 'Portfolio' tab, it will show all the traders you have copied and will summarize your net position in terms of the amount of investment allocated, net profit & loss, and total equity. It is advisable to leave your investment there for a certain period of time, depending on the trader's strategy. Once you are ready to pull out your funds, simply go to the 'Withdraw Funds' tab and get paid! Feel free to research more traders to copy or pull funds out of those who are not performing as expected.

- *CopyPortfolios*

  We have discussed copying individual traders, but you can also invest in CopyPortfolios. This is essentially a similar concept as already discussed, but on a larger scale which requires a larger minimum investment of at least $5,000. CopyPortfolios are aimed towards assisting investors in minimizing their long-term risk, whilst promoting growth opportunities, creating diversified investments. They are essentially investment channels that bundle together a collection of financial assets and are intended for the medium to long-term investment period, but your funds can be withdrawn at any time you choose. There are two types of CopyPortfolios:

  - **Top Trader Portfolios** - these are made up of the best-performing and most sustainable traders on the eToro platform.

  - **Market Portfolios** - these bundle together CFD stocks, ETFs, or commodities under one selected market strategy

Benefits of eToro Copy Trading:

- Allows you to diversify your portfolio very easily

- No experience of financial markets required

- No need to spend hours researching markets

- Leverage other traders' expertise and success

- Learn from the experts, hone your trading skills

- No management fees or other costs involved

- Capital required to start: $200+

- Earning potential: Dependent on the level of investment. The 50 most copied traders for 2020 on eToro had an average yearly profit of 83.7%. This equates to a profit of $837 on $1000 invested, or $8370 profit on $10,000.

- Time spent on business: 5 minutes per day

STEP 3
TAKE ACTION!

"The only impossible journey is the one you never begin."

- Tony Robbins

You are one of the people who have decided to take charge of your life and earn yourself a substantial passive income, whatever that target income may be, the fact you purchased this book means you are already on the path to success.

Now it is time for the grand finale! You have taken the first step and bought the book; you learned and absorbed a lot of information on some simple yet effective strategies to get to $10,000+ per month in passive income, now all that is left is one final step - the most important step - to **take action today!** Not tomorrow, not on the weekend, or next week, but now. There is no time like the present; just focus on moving forward one step at a time, chipping away at your goal in bite-sized chunks. Start with one strategy, take it step-by-step, and before you know it, you will be on your way to $10,000 per month in passive income, working no more than 20 hours a week and getting to enjoy your life more, spending more time with your loved ones.

It may be daunting, it may be scary, and yes, you may fail at some aspects of the process. With failure comes valuable education. There is no success without failure. But even if you do fail to some degree, ask yourself what will you have lost in doing so?

Money?

Hell no! You will not have lost any money as the strategies I have taught you do not involve much capital outlay - in fact, most involve very little to none at all.

Pride?

You will not have lost any pride, as you will have gained a sense of achievement simply by taking action and making a good attempt at it. Some of those around you may think you are crazy for trying something new, something different, which they may not necessarily understand. But if you are dissatisfied with the status quo and don't make a change to what you're doing every day, then you will not see a change in your desired outcome either. Albert Einstein is widely credited with saying, *"The definition of insanity is doing the same thing over and over again, but expecting different results."*

Time?

You will not even have lost much time, as the knowledge & experience you will have gained in simply taking action and learning about each aspect of the process will be invaluable; you will only have added to your skill set.

In fact, by taking action today, you are really only setting up to benefit positively; all you have is to gain. You will gain valuable knowledge and experience. You will have a better platform from which to build yourself and your passive income streams further. All you have to do is keep at it and never give up until you have accomplished each one of your goals.

The simple fact of action puts you ahead of 99% of people. Success is the only outcome of a process that starts with taking action. Without action, it is impossible to attain success. Taking action every day to achieve your goals sets you on the path to achieving success.

CONCLUSION

"You don't have to be great to start, but you do have to start to be great."

- Zig Ziglar

I hope you have enjoyed the journey of learning how to achieve financial freedom through passive income. You now have the basic tools and strategies, in a step-by-step format to apply and implement on your path to success. The key is to identify the strategies, set your goal of what you want to achieve and how you intend to get there, set out a detailed step-by-step action plan, and then simply follow each step diligently. Do not stop until you achieve your goals; you are perfectly capable of achieving $10,000+ in passive income streams without slaving away for hours every day. Work smart, not hard. Make use of other people's time and even other people's money if you have to borrow.

The strategies I have taught you in this book are from proven business models that work in today's market, which I have used and had success with, and which can be implemented immediately. There is no doubt there will be times of hardship and trepidation, but millions of other successful entrepreneurs around the world have achieved success in these businesses; the underlying question is whether or not you take the necessary action today to join them in their success? If the answer is no, there is only one thing stopping you - and that is you! So get your head in the game, and get moving towards $10,000+ in passive income today!

Download your FREE gift from me to you: **110 Passive Income Ideas** at www.jp-clarke.com/bonus

If you enjoyed this book, please take a few seconds to leave an honest review on Amazon; I would love to hear how the book impacted you, even if only a few sentences.

REVIEW
ON AMAZON

If you enjoyed this book, please show your support by leaving a review on Amazon. Reviews are the best way for us to get noticed and are a great way for you to participate in our development.

★ ★ ★ ★ ★

1. **Go to amazon.com/ryp**
   (or scan QR code)
2. **Scroll to your purchase**
3. **Select Star Rating**

REFERENCES

9 out of 10 millionaires created their wealth through real estate. (n.d.). Money Under 30. Retrieved April 1, 2021, from https://www.moneyunder30.com/should-you-invest-in-real-estate-crowdfunding2021 Wholesale Shockproof Tpu Cover. (n.d.). [Photograph]. 2021 Wholesale Shockproof Tpu Cover. https://tomsan.en.alibaba.com/product/62427890588-820581953/2021_Wholesale_Shockproof_TPU_Cover_Cell_Phone_Case_for_iPhone_11_Pr o_Max.html?spm=a2700.shop_plgr.41413.10.d2162287aStSZz2021 Wholesale Shockproof Tpu Cover Cell Phone Case For Iphone 11 Pro Max - Buy Tpu Case For Apple Iphone 7,I Phone Cases,Mobile Phone Bags & Cases Product on Alibaba.com. (n.d.). Alibaba. Retrieved April 1, 2021, from https://tomsan.en.alibaba.com/product/62427890588-820581953/2021_Wholesale_Shockproof_TPU_Cover_Cell_Phone_Case_for_iPhone_11_Pr o_Max.html?spm=a2700.shop_plgr.41413.10.d2162287aStSZzA quote by Anthony Robbins. (n.d.). Good Reads. Retrieved April 1, 2021, from https://www.goodreads.com/quotes/877199-the-only-impossible-journey-is-the-one-you-never-beginA quote by Theodore Roosevelt. (n.d.). Good Reads. Retrieved April 1, 2021, from https://www.goodreads.com/quotes/1311039-there-can-be-no-life-without-change-and-to-beA quote from Andrew Carnegie. (n.d.). Good Reads. Retrieved April 1, 2021, from https://www.goodreads.com/quotes/9118668-ninety-percent-of-all-millionaires-become-so-through-owing-realA quote from Think and Grow Rich. (n.d.). Good Reads. Retrieved April 1, 2021, from https://www.goodreads.com/quotes/77253-whatever-the-mind-can-conceive-and-believe-it-can-achieveAmazon.com. (n.d.). Fulfillment by Amazon (FBA) | How It Works. Amazon. Retrieved April 1, 2021, from https://sell.amazon.com/fulfillment-by-amazon.htmlAmazon.com: SURPHY Silicone Case. (n.d.). [Photograph]. Amazon.Com: SURPHY Silicone Case. https://www.amazon.com/SURPHY-Silicone-Compatible-Thickening-Microfiber/dp/B07WJZBX3T/ref=sr_1_6?dchild=1&keywords=surphy&qid=1617259584&ref resh=1&sr=8-6Amazon.com: SURPHY Silicone Case Compatible with iPhone 11 Pro Max Case 6.5 inches, Liquid Silicone Full Body Thickening Design Phone Case (with Microfiber Lining) for 11 Pro Max 2019 (Yellow). (n.d.). Amazon.Com|SURPHY. Retrieved April 1, 2021, from https://www.amazon.com/SURPHY-Silicone-Compatible-Thickening-Microfiber/dp/B07WJZBX3T/ref=sr_1_6?dchild=1&keywords=surphy&qid=1617259584&ref resh=1&sr=8-6Benjamin Franklin Quotes. (n.d.). BrainyQuote. Retrieved April 1, 2021, from https://www.brainyquote.com/quotes/benjamin_franklin_141119Chanter, T. (2019, July 23). "Creativity doesn't wait for that perfect moment. - Tom Chanter. Medium. https://medium.com/@tomchanter/creativity-doesnt-wait-for-that-perfect-moment-82b90aa63aaChoa, L. (2017, June 7). Ignoring online marketing is like opening a business but not telling anyone. Content Maximiser. https://contentmaximiser.com/marketing-monday-44/ignoring-online-marketing-is-like-opening-a-business-but-not-telling-anyone/Crowd, L. (2016, April 7). A brief history of crowdfunding. LendingCrowd. https://www.lendingcrowd.com/blog/a-brief-history-of-crowdfunding#:%7E:text=The%20first%20incidence%20of%20modern,to%20fund%20their %20US%20tourDayton, E. (2021, January 26). Amazon Statistics You Should Know: Opportunities to Make the Most of America's Top Online Marketplace. The BigCommerce Blog. https://www.bigcommerce.co.uk/blog/amazon-statistics/#10-fascinating-amazon-statistics-sellers-need-to-know-in-2020FBA Revenue Calculator. (n.d.). [Photograph]. FBA Revenue Calculator. https://sellercentral.amazon.com/hz/fba/profitabilitycalculator/index?lang=en_USFulfillme nt by Amazon Revenue Calculator. (n.d.). Amazon FBA Revenue Calculator. Retrieved April 1, 2021, from https://sellercentral.amazon.com/hz/fba/profitabilitycalculator/index?lang=en_USGodin, M. (2019, January 31). From Zero to $1M in 8 Months | Awesome Dropshipping Success Stories. EBay Sellers Journey to $100,000 a Month. https://crazylister.com/blog/dropshipping-success-stories/How Much Is the Average Salary for U.S. Workers? (n.d.). The Balance Careers. Retrieved April 1, 2021, from https://www.thebalancecareers.com/average-salary-information-for-us-workers-2060808Junglescout Sales Data - SURPHY. (n.d.). [Photograph].

Junglescout. https://www.amazon.com/SURPHY-Silicone-Compatible-Thickening-Microfiber/dp/B07WJZBX3T/ref=sr_1_6?dchild=1&keywords=surphy&qid=1617260044&sr=8-6Labatt-Simon, C. (2021, March 30). Leveraging Amazon FBA for Your Online Sales Success. The BigCommerce Blog. https://www.bigcommerce.co.uk/blog/amazon-fba/Lee Bolman Quote: A vision without a strategy remains an illusion. (n.d.). Quote Fancy. Retrieved April 1, 2021, from https://quotefancy.com/quote/1718862/Lee-Bolman-A-vision-without-a-strategy-remains-an-illusionMohsin, M. (2021, March 17). 10 Amazon Statistics You Need to Know in 2021 [March 2021]. Oberlo. https://www.oberlo.co.uk/blog/amazon-statisticsMooshe. (n.d.). Mooshe Socks - Case Study. Retrieved April 1, 2021, from https://shopmooshesocks.comPatel, N. (2020, January 23). A Brief Guide to Designing High-Converting Landing Pages. Neil Patel. https://neilpatel.com/blog/a-brief-guide-to-designing-high-converting-landing-pages/Rose, J. (2020, December 16). How To Make Over $100,000 Per Year Creating Online Courses. Forbes. https://www.forbes.com/sites/jrose/2017/09/12/how-to-make-over-100000-per-year-creating-online-courses/?sh=2735f6842157Sayner, A. (2020, August 19). How Much Can You Make Selling Online Courses? Online Course How. https://www.onlinecoursehow.com/tips/how-much-can-you-make-selling-online-courses/#:%7E:text=Your%20online%20course%20could%20earn,earn%20by%20selling%20online%20coursesSuccess at the highest level comes down to one question: Can you decide that your happiness can come from someone else's success? Bill Walton. (n.d.). Quote Master. Retrieved April 1, 2021, from https://www.quotemaster.org/qe31d2f47220bbf7e2c693278c246d930Velyka, D. (2021, February 26). Dropship From Wayfair: The Ultimate Guide 2021. Dropship Academy. https://blog.dsmtool.com/dropshipping-suppliers/dropship-from-wayfair-guide/#is-wayfair-a-dropshipperWarren Buffett Quote: If you don't find a way to make money while you sleep, you will work until you die. (n.d.). Quote Fancy. Retrieved April 1, 2021, from https://quotefancy.com/quote/930999/Warren-Buffett-If-you-don-t-find-a-way-to-make-money-while-you-sleep-you-will-work-untilZig Ziglar Quotes. (n.d.). BrainyQuote. Retrieved April 1, 2021, from https://www.brainyquote.com/quotes/zig_ziglar_617778Ziglar, T. (2016, July 25). You don't build a business. Ziglar Inc. https://www.ziglar.com/articles/dont-build-business/

Tony Robbins Quotes. (n.d.). BrainyQuote. Retrieved April 2, 2021, from https://www.brainyquote.com/quotes/tony_robbins_147805?src=t_copy

Copy top-performing traders with eToro's CopyTraderTM. (2021, March 16). EToro Statistics. https://www.etoro.com/copytrader/

eToro CopyPortfolios. (n.d.). EToro CopyPortfolios. Retrieved April 2, 2021, from https://www.etoro.com/investing/copyportfolios/

eToro Average Yearly Profit 83.7% for 2020. (n.d.). [Photograph]. EToro Average Yearly Profit 83.7% for 2020. https://www.etoro.com/copytrader/

eToro Popular Investor Profile - HarryH1993. (n.d.). [Photograph]. eToro Popular Investor Profile - HarryH1993. https://www.etoro.com/people/harryh1993/stats

Hamm, T. (2020, November 12). If You Want Different Results, You Have to Try Different Approaches. The Simple Dollar. https://www.thesimpledollar.com/make-money/if-you-want-different-results-you-have-to-try-different-approaches/

Made in United States
Troutdale, OR
05/31/2023

10350874R10049